GREAT MINDS® WIT & WISDOM

Grade 7 Module 4:
Fever

Student Edition

COPYRIGHT STATEMENT

Published by Great Minds®.

Copyright ©2017 Great Minds®. All rights reserved. No part of this work may be reproduced or used in any form or by any means—graphic, electronic, or mechanical, including photocopying or information storage and retrieval systems—without written permission from the copyright holder.

ISBN: 978-1-68386-048-8

Table of Contents

Handout 1A: Research Overview

Handout 2A: Character Analysis

Handout 2B: Fluency Homework

Handout 3A: Historical Details in Fiction and Nonfiction

Handout 3B: Content-Specific Words

Handout 5A: Different Types of Adjectives

Handout 6A: Coordinate and Compound Adjectives

Handout 7A: Yellow Fever Epidemic Details

Handout 8A: Chapter 10 Character Details

Handout 8B: Credible vs. Non-Credible Sources

Handout 8C: Words with the Root *cred*

Handout 9A: Coordinate and Compound Adjectives

Handout 13A: Analysis of Mattie

Handout 13B: Fluency Homework

Handout 14A: "Yellow Fever" Article Summary

Handout 14B: Simile Interpretation

Handout 15A: Comparison of Presentation Visuals

Handout 15B: Sample Presentation Plan

Handout 16A: Impact of Individuals

Handout 17A: Girard's Film Depiction

Handout 18A: Fluency Homework

Handout 19A: Tableau Planning Sheet

Handout 19B: Informal vs. Formal Language

Handout 20A: Presentation Planning Tool

Handout 24A: Free African Society Notes

Handout 25A: "Invictus" Analysis

Handout 25B: Research Essay Model

Handout 25C: Fluency Homework

Handout 27A: Speaking and Listening Goal-Setting and Self-Assessment

Handout 28A: Character Analysis

Handout 29A: Illness Words

Handout 30A: Aftermath Analysis

Handout 31A: Speaking and Listening Goal-Setting and Self-Assessment

Handout 32A: Focusing Question Task 3 Organizer

Handout 33A: End-of-Module Task Evidence

Handout 34A: End-of-Module Task Evidence

Handout 34B: Works Cited Guide

Handout 37A: Informative Essay Checklist

Handout 38A: Speaking and Listening Goal-Setting and Self-Assessment

Volume of Reading Reflection Questions

Wit & Wisdom Parent Tip Sheet

Name _____

Date _____ Class _____

Handout 1A: Research Overview

Directions: Use Section 1 as a reference to the key steps of the research process. Use Section 2 to take notes as you engage in research yourself. Then, keep this handout as a reference when you complete further research and the End-of-Module Task.

Section 1: Overview

- Step 1: Identify a topic and ask a research question.
- Step 2: Seek information to answer the question.
- Step 3: Evaluate sources.
- Step 4: Read and take notes.
- Step 5: Synthesize research findings.
- Step 6: Incorporate and credit sources.
- Step 7: Share the research.

*Note that researchers do not always complete the steps in this order and may return to earlier steps as they find new information.

Section 2: Steps

Step 1: Identify a Topic and Ask a Research Question

Notes about crafting an effective research question:

_____
_____
_____
_____
_____
_____

My research topic for Lessons 1 to 12 is:

_____

_____

My research question for Lessons 1 to 12 is:

_____

_____

_____

_____

Name _____

Date _____ Class _____

Step 2: Seek Information to Answer the Question

Tips for Identifying Sources

- Seek print sources (books, magazines, newspapers, journals), electronic sources (Internet search engines, videos), visual sources (photographs, maps), or field research (historical buildings, museums, or other locations).
- Use the index of print sources.
- Look at others' bibliographies in print sources.
- Use the school or local library.
- Identify search terms for online searches.

Guidelines for effective search terms:

_____

_____

_____

Lesson 5 search activity notes:

- The selected research question:

    _____

    _____

- The search terms used:

    _____

    _____

- The selected site (by name and web address or source):

    _____

    _____

- Explain why this site seems helpful to answering the research question.

_____

_____

_____

Notes on finding sources:

_____

_____

_____

_____

Notes on possible sources for my research question:

_____

_____

_____

_____

_____

_____

_____

Name: _____

Date: _____ Class: _____

Step 3: Evaluate Sources

It is important to evaluate the sources you find.

Notes on guidelines for evaluating sources:

- Domain: _____

- Author: _____

- Publisher: _____

- Date: _____

- Sources: _____

- Facts: _____

- Purpose: _____

- Other: _____

Lesson 9 example of a credible source (and explanation):

_____
_____
_____

Lesson 9 example of a non-credible source (and explanation):

_____
_____
_____

Step 4: Read and Take Notes

Once you have sources that are credible and relevant, read them and take notes.

Lesson 10 notes on note-taking:

_____
_____
_____
_____
_____

Remember: NEVER copy word for word unless you are quoting from a source. Be sure to avoid plagiarism by always quoting or crediting your sources.

Notes on your topic/research question for Lessons 1 to 12:

_____
_____
_____
_____
_____
_____
_____
_____

Name _____

Date _____ Class _____

Step 5: Synthesize Research Findings

Once you have collected information from credible sources, begin to make sense of your research findings by synthesizing it or bringing it all together.

Lesson 23 notes on synthesizing:

_____
_____
_____
_____
_____
_____
_____
_____
_____
_____
_____

Step 6: Incorporate and Credit Sources

Remember: NEVER copy word for word unless you are quoting from a source. Be sure to avoid plagiarism by quoting or crediting sources.

Lesson 17 notes on quoting, paraphrasing, and summarizing:

Quoting:

_____

_____

_____

_____

Paraphrasing:

_____

_____

_____

_____

Summarizing:

_____

_____

_____

_____

Name

Date   Class

Notes on citing sources from Deep Dive 25 and Lesson 27:

Step 7: Share the Research

After you have done your research and synthesized the information, it's time to share it! For example, you might make a formal presentation about your research or write a research essay. You may want to include charts, visuals, or graphics to illustrate key points within either as well.

Lessons 13 and 14 notes on what makes a presentation effective:

_____
_____
_____
_____
_____
_____
_____
_____
_____

Name _____
Date _____ Class _____

Lesson 15 notes on Dos and Don'ts of effective visuals:

Do	Don't

Lesson 25 notes on characteristics of a research essay:

Lesson 30 notes on formatting within a research essay:

Handout 2A: Character Analysis

Directions: What do we know about Mattie and her mother after reading through chapter 3 of *Fever 1793*? Complete the table with textual evidence and your own analysis of the characters.

	What do we know about Mattie?	…about Mother?	…about their relationship?
What the Text Says: **Details from the Text**			
What the Text Means: **Analysis of the Text**			

Handout 2B: Fluency Homework

Directions:

1. Day 1: Read the text carefully, and annotate to help you read fluently.
2. Each day:
    a. Practice reading the text aloud three to five times.
    b. Evaluate your progress by placing a check mark in the appropriate unshaded box.
    c. Ask someone (adult or peer) to listen and evaluate you as well.
3. Last day: Respond to the self-reflection questions at the end of this handout.

"She was my friend! You must allow me. Why are you so horrid?"

As soon as the angry words were out of my mouth, I knew I had gone too far.

"Matilda!" Mother rose from her chair. "You are forbidden to speak to me in that tone! Apologize at once."

The sun coming in the south window cast deep shadows under her eyes and cheekbones. She held her jaw tight, her eyes flashing with anger. She looked old, much older than she should. She hadn't always been so pinch-faced and harsh.

When mother allowed herself a still moment by the fire on winter nights, I could sometimes see the face she wore when Father was alive. Back then Mother smiled at me with her eyes and her laughter and her gentle hands. But no longer. Life was a battle, and Mother a tired and bitter captain. The captain I had to obey.

"My apologies," I said.

Anderson, Laurie Halse. *Fever 1793.* Simon & Schuster, 2000, pp. 16–17.

Student Performance Checklist:	Day 1		Day 2		Day 3		Day 4		Day 5	
	You	Listener*	You	Listener*	You	Listener*	You	Listener*	You	Listener*
Accurately read the passage three to five times.										
Read with appropriate phrasing and pausing.										
Read with appropriate expression.										
Read articulately at a good pace and an audible volume.										

*Adult or peer

Self-reflection: What choices did you make when deciding how to read this passage, and why? What would you like to improve on or try differently next time?

Handout 3A: Historical Details in Fiction and Nonfiction

Directions: How does Anderson use historical details to create her fictional account in *Fever 1793*? Locate and cite quotations or historical facts from *An American Plague* in the first column. Then, describe how that historical fact is portrayed in *Fever 1793* in the second column. Some second-column possibilities include:

- The narrator's thoughts.
- Dialogue between characters.
- The narrator's description of what she sees, hears, or smells.

Fact from *An American Plague* Shown in *Fever 1793*	How That Historical Fact Is Portrayed in *Fever 1793*

	How That Historical Fact Is Portrayed in *Fever 1793*
Fact from *An American Plague* Shown in *Fever 1793*	

Name _____

Date _____ Class _____

	How That Historical Fact Is Portrayed in *Fever 1793*
Fact from *An American Plague* Shown in *Fever 1793*	

Fact from *An American Plague* Shown in *Fever 1793*	How That Historical Fact Is Portrayed in *Fever 1793*

	Fact from *An American Plague* Shown in *Fever 1793*	How That Historical Fact Is Portrayed in *Fever 1793*

Name _____

Date _____ Class _____

Handout 3B: Content-Specific Words

Directions: The words below appear in chapter 1 of *An American Plague*, and are used to set the scene for the coming epidemic. Add definitions for the words in your category.

Categories and Words	Part of Speech	Definition
Business and Trade Words		
cargo (2)		
vendors (3)		
wharf (3)		
wares (3)		
manufacturer (3)		
Community and Society Words		
inhabitants (3)		
citizens (5)		
residents (9)		
authorities (9)		
population (9)		

Categories and Words	Part of Speech	Definition
Politics and Government Words		
capital (4)		
federal (government) (4)		
monarch (4)		
republic (5)		
oppression (5)		
Weather and Environment Words		
unrelenting (sun) (1)		
humid (1)		
runoff (2)		
sweltering (3)		
drought (6)		

Handout 5A: Different Types of Adjectives

Directions: Review the following examples of different types of adjectives from *An American Plague*, noting which type of adjectives is used in each sentence. Then, when prompted, complete the Exit Ticket.

Examples from *An American Plague*	Type
Mosquitoes' "high-pitched whirring was particularly loud" (1).	
"Washington spent the day at home in a small, stuffy office" (4).	
"Pro-French sympathies were further heightened" (5).	
"One of the many narrow, forgotten alleys of Philadelphia" (8).	
"[C]ity, state, and federal governments went about their business" (9).	
"It was clear that thirty-three-year-old Catherine LeMaigre was dying" (11).	
"[H]er skin took on the pale-yellow color that gave the disease its name" (12).	
"Rush was forty-seven years old" (12).	
"[T]he patient vomited stale, black blood" (14).	
"Philadelphia was in the grip of a deadly, unstoppable plague" (16).	
"[T]hrough it all a single, chilling sound could still be heard–the awful tolling of the church bells" (19).	

Exit Ticket:

Read the following two examples. In the space before each sentence, label each as containing either coordinate or compound adjectives. Then, on the lines below each sentence, describe the purpose that the adjectives serve.

_____ "… Mother turned her attention to the most important issue–<u>tea-drinking</u> clothes. We had <u>tea-buying</u> clothes, <u>tea-brewing</u> clothes, and <u>tea-serving</u> clothes, but we had no <u>taking-tea-with-the-Ogilvies</u> clothes" (Anderson 42).

_____

_____

_____

_____ "The city's taverns buzzed with the talk of the <u>strange, killing</u> fever" (Murphy 18).

_____

_____

_____

Handout 6A: Coordinate and Compound Adjectives

Part 1 Directions: Read each sentence. Then, fill in each blank or replace the underlined portions of the sentences with either coordinate or compound adjectives to more fully and precisely describe each person, place, or thing. Then, in the second column, explain how your additions improve the sentence.

	How do the adjectives improve the sentence?
All of the citizens of Philadelphia were complaining of the _____ air (that was foul smelling).	
The victims of the plague vomited _____ bile.	
Mattie wore a _____ shift (that was soaked with sweat) to the Ogilvies' house.	
Even though she was relatively young and healthy, _____ Catherine LeMaigre (who was thirty-three years old) died of yellow fever.	
People in Philadelphia would start to panic as they learned more of the _____ disease.	

Part 2 Directions: Write three sentences to describe the characters at or the setting of the Ogilvies' tea party from chapter 7 of *Fever* 1793. Use at least one set of correctly punctuated coordinate or compound adjectives in each sentence, and be sure to include at least one example of each type.

Sentence 1:

_____

_____

_____

Sentence 2:

_____

_____

_____

Sentence 3:

_____

_____

_____

Handout 7A: Yellow Fever Epidemic Details

Directions: Add quotations, ideas, and details from chapters 8 and 9 of *Fever 1793* on each of the topics listed below.

The Spread of the Epidemic in the City	People's Reactions and Attempts to Respond	The Symptoms of the Disease	How Doctors (and Others) Treated Those with the Disease

Handout 8A: Chapter 10 Character Details

Directions: Complete the chart to show the character developments and responses to the crisis.

Character	What He or She Is Thinking, Doing, or Saying in Chapter 10	How These Developments Are a Response to the Increasing Crisis
Mattie		
Grandfather		
Mother		

Character	What He or She Is Thinking, Doing, or Saying in Chapter 10	How These Developments Are a Response to the Increasing Crisis
Doctor Kerr		
Nathaniel Benson		
Master Peale (the Painter)		

Name _____

Date _____ Class _____

Handout 8B: Credible vs. Non-Credible Sources

Directions: Finding accurate, reliable, credible sources is essential for researchers to be confident in their findings. Think about how to determine if a research source is accurate and reliable. Look at each of the descriptions of the sources below, and:

- Identify if it is probably credible; might be credible but you would need more information; or does not seem credible.
- Explain why you rated it that way, and how it could be used in research about the yellow fever epidemic of 1793.

The first one has been done for you as an example.

Possible Research Source	Probably Credible	Might Be Credible	Not Credible	Why did you give this rating, and how could this source be used in research about the yellow fever epidemic of 1793?
A Philadelphia history blog from a well-known history professor from a respected university (from a site with a .edu domain name).	✓			*Even though this is a blog, the author is known and respected. This might be a source for historical facts and information about the city.*
A personal blog from a Philadelphian who leads tours in Philadelphia of places that were mentioned in the book *Fever 1793* (from a site with a .org domain name).				
A web page on yellow fever from the Centers for Disease Control and Prevention (CDC), which is the leading national public health institution (from a site with a .gov domain name).				

Possible Research Source	Probably Credible	Might Be Credible	Not Credible	Why did you give this rating, and how could this source be used in research about the yellow fever epidemic of 1793?
A social media post from a person who survived a modern-day yellow fever outbreak, describing how awful the disease was.				
A historical fiction novel set in Philadelphia in the 1790s.				
A letter from George Washington to his wife, describing the fever outbreak and explaining why he was leaving the city of Philadelphia.				
A letter written by a real-life person who was like Mrs. Ogilvie in *Fever 1793*, who wrote to her sister, explaining why her family would never get the fever because it only affected poor people who lived by the water.				

Name _____

Date _____ Class _____

Possible Research Source	Probably Credible	Might Be Credible	Not Credible	Why did you give this rating, and how could this source be used in research about the yellow fever epidemic of 1793?
A description of the yellow fever outbreak of 1793 from a website that is a free encyclopedia, written anonymously by the people who read it (from a site with a .org domain name).				
Information about Philadelphia and its history and historic buildings from a company that leads tours of historic Philadelphia (from a site with a .com domain name).				
A book about the yellow fever epidemic of 1793 that is published by a well-known publisher and includes ten pages of research sources in the back of the book.				
A document about the fever written by the Historical Society of Pennsylvania, which is one of the oldest historical societies in the country and maintains a large collection of historical documents and images.				

Possible Research Source	Probably Credible	Might Be Credible	Not Credible	Why did you give this rating, and how could this source be used in research about the yellow fever epidemic of 1793?
A blog from a teacher.				

Name _____

Date _____ Class _____

Handout 8C: Words with the Root *cred*

Part 1 Directions: Read each word, the word in context, and the definitions for the word parts. Then, write your own definition for each word on the lines provided.

incredible—It seems <u>incredible</u> that doctors in Philadelphia believed that the yellow fever was caused by a bad smell and that bleeding was a good treatment for the disease.

in- = not

-ible = able to be

Definition for *incredible*:

_____

_____

_____

discredit—The work of researchers who found that illness was caused by tiny organisms, such as bacteria and viruses, would ultimately <u>discredit</u> earlier doctors who thought that sickness was the result of one's humors being out of balance.

dis- = the negative of; the reverse of

Definition for *discredit*:

_____

_____

_____

Part 2 Directions: Read about each word, and then complete the sentences about each word.

credo—A credo is like a motto, a statement of belief. Boxer's motto was "I will work harder."

credibility—The suffix *-ibility/-ability* means "the state or condition of being able; the quality of, ability to, or suitability for a certain action."

credit—Buying something on credit means that the store or business lets you pay for it later.

1. The Mayor's credo might be _____.

   _____

   _____

2. Credibility is important in research sources because _____.

   _____

   _____

3. If the Cooks allowed someone to buy something on credit at the coffeehouse, how does their action connect to the root's meaning of "belief"?

   _____

   _____

Handout 9A: Coordinate and Compound Adjectives

Directions: Add punctuation to the underlined adjectives in each sentence, name the type of adjectives used in the sentence, and then explain the purpose of the adjectives in the sentence.

	Type
The yellow fever spread quickly in Philadelphia because of the <u>hot humid</u> weather and the <u>narrow crowded</u> streets.	
Her mother was like a <u>tired bitter</u> captain who Mattie had to obey.	
When Mattie went to the market, she bought some <u>sweet tasting</u> lemons that left a <u>bitter sweet long lasting</u> taste in her mouth.	
Mattie had to wear an <u>old fashioned</u> dress to tea.	
When Eliza looked at her with a <u>stony faced</u> expression, Mattie realized she would not be able to convince her that she should stay.	
Grandfather dressed as a soldier to show that he would protect Mattie from the <u>dreaded terrible</u> enemy, yellow fever.	

Handout 13A: Analysis of Mattie

Directions: Complete the chart with evidence from chapters 11 and 12 and your own inferences. Then answer the question that follows.

Examples from the Text	What the Example Reveals about Mattie
What Mattie thinks.	
What Mattie does.	
What Mattie says.	
What others say to or about Mattie.	

Use the evidence you selected to explain how and why Mattie is changing and how her relationship with her grandfather also changes as a result.

_____
_____
_____
_____
_____
_____

Handout 13B: Fluency Homework

Directions:

1. Day 1: Read the text carefully, and annotate to help you read fluently.
2. Each day:
   a. Practice reading the text aloud three to five times.
   b. Evaluate your progress by placing a checkmark in the appropriate unshaded box.
   c. Ask someone (adult or peer) to listen and evaluate you as well.
3. Last day: Respond to the self-reflection questions at the end of this handout.

"There," he sighed. "That's better. It's time to review your soldiering lessons."

I groaned. From my crawling days, Grandfather had taught me all the tricks of the American and the British armies, and quite a few from the French. Again and again and again. It would do no good to argue. I was his captive.

"A soldier needs three things to fight," he continued. He held up three fingers and waited for my response.

"One, a sturdy pair of boots," I said. "Two, a full belly. Three, a decent night's sleep."

Grandfather thunked his boots on the floorboards.

"Hey," protested the farmer.

"My boots are sound."

Grandfather belched.

"Tsk, tsk," said the farmer's wife.

"Eliza fed me breakfast enough for two blacksmiths."

He pulled the brim of his hat down over his eyes and settled back against a rolled-up mattress.

Anderson, Laurie Halse. *Fever 1793*. Simon & Schuster, 2000, pp. 79–80.

Student Performance Checklist:	Day 1		Day 2		Day 3		Day 4		Day 5	
	You	Listener*	You	Listener*	You	Listener*	You	Listener*	You	Listener*
Accurately read the passage three to five times.										
Read with appropriate phrasing and pausing.										
Read with appropriate expression.										
Read articulately at a good pace and an audible volume.										

*Adult or peer

Self-reflection: What choices did you make when deciding how to read this passage and why? What would you like to improve on or try differently next time?

Handout 14A: "Yellow Fever" Article Summary

Directions: Work with others who have the same assigned section to complete the chart by defining at least two unknown vocabulary words from your section, writing the main idea for the section, and then noting key details. Then work with your original small group to write a summary of the article as a whole in the last row of the chart.

Section 1: Causes	Vocabulary: word 1 plus definition
	Vocabulary: word 2 plus definition
	Main idea
	Key detail
	Key detail

Section 2: Symptoms	Vocabulary: word 1 plus definition
	Vocabulary: word 2 plus definition
	Main idea
	Key detail 1
	Key detail 2

Name _____

Date _____ Class _____

Section 3: Exams and Tests; Treatment	Vocabulary: word 1 plus definition
	Vocabulary: word 2 plus definition
	Main idea
	Key detail 1
	Key detail 2

Section 4: Outlook (Prognosis); Possible Complications	Vocabulary: word 1 plus definition
	Vocabulary: word 2 plus definition
	Main idea
	Key detail 1
	Key detail 2

Name _____

Date _____ Class _____

Section 5: When to Contact a Medical Professional; Prevention; Alternative Names	Vocabulary: word 1 plus definition
	Vocabulary: word 2 plus definition
	Main idea
	Key detail 1
	Key detail 2

Article as a Whole	Write a one-sentence summary of the article.
	What is the central idea of the article, and how do the different sections contribute to that central idea?

Handout 14B: Simile Interpretation

Directions: Work with a partner to analyze each simile by answering each of the questions on the chart.

Figurative Language from Chapter 13 of *Fever 1793*	What two things are being compared?	What does the comparison show?	What does the simile show about Mattie's point of view?
1. "Why couldn't I have acted strong and calm like Eliza instead of blubbering like a baby? I disgusted Mother. She knew I was weak" (89).			
2. "The sun was at its highest as I set out on my search. It felt like a bonfire spitting embers on my head" (93).			
3. "The heat rolled to the horizon like waves toward shore" (94).			

Handout 15A: Comparison of Presentation Visuals

Directions: When directed, think about how the slide in the "Do" column would help a presentation. Then think about why that slide would be more effective than the ones in the "Don't" columns.

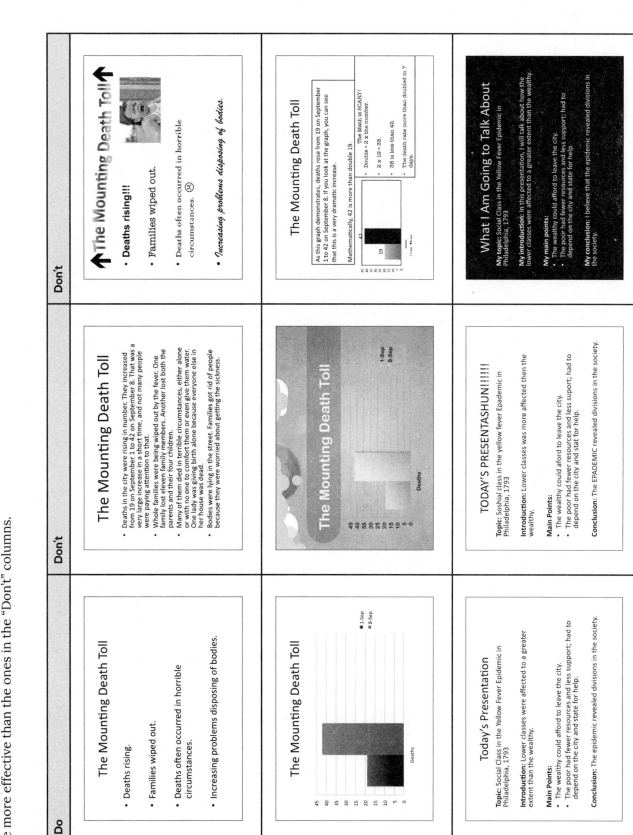

Handout 15B: Sample Presentation Plan

Directions: Imagine you are making a presentation about the government's response to the crisis, and these are your notes with your ideas about what to say. Make a visual that would support one or more parts of a presentation based on the notes.

The Response of the Government to the Crisis	
Introduction: How I Plan to Start My Presentation	**Hook:** When an epidemic or other crisis occurs, we expect the government to step in and help its citizens, right? Well, that's not what happened for most government leaders in Philadelphia in 1793. **Introducing the Topic:** What did most government leaders do? They cowered in fear, passed ineffective laws, abdicated their responsibilities, and left town. **Thesis:** Their cowardice and failure to act led to incredible suffering, mounting problems, and even death for many Philadelphians.

Body: What Ideas I Want to Include in My Presentation	**Key Ideas:**
	- Fear:
	  - Governor is in a "panic" (35).
	  - After their own doorkeeper dies and Dr. Rush says the best advice is to avoid an infected person, the senators and representatives are "unsettled" (36).
	- Ineffective measures:
	  - Order the shooting of a cannon in the streets.
	  - Pass some resolutions like one blaming those from the West Indies for bringing the fever.
	  - Pass a quarantine act.
	- Then, they left! State legislature handed power to governor; governor turned problem to Clarkson. They did not give him any extra funds.
	- Citizens needed help:
	  - More paupers.
	  - More sick.
	  - No food from farmers.
	  - No place to care for sick; no one to care for them.
	  - More people dying.

Conclusion: How I Plan to End My Presentation	At a time when their citizens most needed them, many government officials just walked away and took care of themselves. They left behind poor, sick, and dying people in excruciatingly horrendous conditions.

Handout 16A: Impact of Individuals

Directions: Work with others who have the same assigned person to complete your row of the chart. Then work with your original small group to fill in the rest of the chart and write the central idea of the chapter and a few sentences about how Murphy uses the sections to develop that central idea.

	Who (What information does Murphy provide about these people?)	What (What were the responses of these people to the crisis?)	How (How does Murphy portray them? Cite two specific examples of language Murphy uses and explain the meaning of each.)
Example (done as class): Volunteer Committee (68–69)			
1. Israel Israel (69–70)			
2. Peter Helm (71–72)			

3. Stephen Girard (72–74)	4. Dr. Deveze (74–76)	5. Neighboring communities (76–77)

Name

Date   Class

Based on the sections above, what is a central idea Murphy develops in this chapter?	How does he develop this idea through the sections devoted to individuals?

Name _____

Date _____ Class _____

Handout 17A: Girard's Film Depiction

Directions: As you watch, take notes in the first box on how the filmmakers shape their depiction of Stephen Girard. Then, when directed, place a star next to the most important details, and answer the question at the bottom of the chart.

What details does the film include to shape its presentation of Stephen Girard?

Based on these details, write one sentence to summarize the film's overall depiction of Girard.

Handout 18A: Fluency Homework

Directions:

1. Day 1: Read the text carefully, and annotate to help you read fluently.
2. Each day:
   a. Practice reading the text aloud three to five times.
   b. Evaluate your progress by placing a check mark in the appropriate unshaded box.
   c. Ask someone (adult or peer) to listen and evaluate you as well.
3. Last day: Respond to the self-reflection questions at the end of this handout.

How could the city have changed so much? Yellow fever was wrestling the life out of Philadelphia, infecting the cobblestones, the trees, the nature of the people. Was I living through another nightmare?

"What date is this?" I asked Mrs. Bowles.

"Today is September the twenty-fourth," she answered.

"The twenty-fourth? That's not possible." I counted on my fingers. We fled on the eighth. "When we left, there were reports of a thousand dead. Do you know what the total is now?"

"It's double that at least," she said. "It slowed down those few cool days, but as soon as the temperature rose again, so did the number of corpses."

The driver pulled on his reins to stop the horses. The road was blocked by a line of slow-moving carts, each pushed by a man with a rag tied over his face, each holding a corpse.

"The Potter's Field is ahead," Mrs. Bowles said as she pointed to the front of the line. "That's where they're burying most of the dead. The preachers say a prayer, and someone throws a layer of dirt on top."

Anderson, Laurie Halse. *Fever 1793*. Simon & Schuster, 2000, pp. 119–120.

Student Performance Checklist:	Day 1		Day 2		Day 3		Day 4		Day 5	
	You	Listener*	You	Listener*	You	Listener*	You	Listener*	You	Listener*
Accurately read the passage three to five times.										
Read with appropriate phrasing and pausing.										
Read with appropriate expression.										
Read articulately at a good pace and an audible volume.										

*Adult or peer

Self-reflection: What choices did you make when deciding how to read this passage, and why? What would you like to improve on or try differently next time?

Handout 19A: Tableau Planning Sheet

Directions: Plan a precise tableau that represents the characters' perspectives at this moment.

	What should the character's positioning and facial expression look like?	Explanation for the character's pose: What are they feeling, and what is their motivation?	What technique(s) does Anderson use to convey the character's perspective? (Use evidence.)
Mattie			Example 1: Example 2:
Grandfather			Example 1: Example 2:

Name _____

Date _____ Class _____

	What should the character's positioning and facial expression look like?	Explanation for the character's pose: What are they feeling, and what is their motivation?	What technique(s) does Anderson use to convey the character's perspective? (Use evidence.)
Tall Man			Example 1: Example 2:
Short Man			Example 1: Example 2:

Name _____

Date _____ Class _____

Select a quote to be your tableau's caption:

_____
_____
_____

Explain what the tableau and caption reveal about Mattie, Grandfather, or the effects of the crisis.

_____
_____
_____
_____
_____

Handout 19B: Informal vs. Formal Language

Directions: In Section 1 of the Handout, record examples of errors people make in formal presentations. (Use examples from your experience or from a comparison of the presentation examples below.)

Then, when directed, record presentation issues that may be challenges for you in the first column in Section 2, and record strategies in the second column.

Formal Presentation Example:

I came to Australia to study the deadliest animal in the world. Now there may be some Australian audience members thinking, "Strewth, scientists have finally recognized the importance of the drop bear." But, I'm not studying drop bears because around the world by transmitting deadly diseases, malaria and dengue fever, mosquitoes kill about a million people a year, making them the deadliest animal in the world. Now in Australia the most common mosquito borne disease is Ross River virus, and it occurs at high rates in some areas but not others. My question is why. What is it about certain areas that makes them breed disease?

Johnston, Emily. "2014 Three Minute Thesis winning presentation by Emily Johnston." *YouTube*, uploaded by University of South Australia, 18 Sept. 2014, Web. Accessed 6 Dec. 2016.

Example with Informal Style:

Me and my team came to Australia to study the most awesome, deadliest, and totally cool animal in the whole world. Man, you Australian dudes might think I was talkin' about the drop bear. But, that's not what I wanna talk about. Nope. The animal I studied is super tiny but goes around the world spreading deadly diseases, and we gotta stop it, it's so deadly. Yep, you got it—it's the mosquito. Those bugs go around spreading germs that cause people to get sick. And those sicknesses kill a huge amount of people like every year. So, um, that's why I came to Australia. Just so you know, the Australian mosquito spreads a germ called the Ross River virus, but they don't just do it the same everywhere. They spread it more in some places than other places. So that's what I've been wondering about. Why do these guys spread the virus more in some spots than other ones? What's up with that?

Section 1

Type of error	Example(s)
Imprecise vocabulary	
Informal vocabulary or slang	
Meaningless words	
Incorrect pronunciation or failure to clearly enunciate words	
Grammatical errors	
Other	

Name _____

Date _____ Class _____

Section 2

Possible Solutions				
Issues I Struggle With				

Handout 20A: Presentation Planning Tool

Directions: Use the following tool to plan your presentation. (Remember: You do not need to plan in the order of the presentation elements listed on this handout. In fact, you may want to begin by planning the body of the presentation before planning the introduction or conclusion. However, your final presentation should include all the elements contained on this tool.)

Introduction

		Ideas for Visuals for Your Introduction:
Hook Your Audience	What will you say to catch your audience's attention?	
Introduce Your Topic	How will you introduce your presentation topic or research question?	
State Your Thesis	What is the essential idea or point about your question or topic you want to convey?	

Body of Presentation*

For each idea, write notes for how you will state the idea, what evidence or examples you will provide, and how you might elaborate on those. Also include notes about any visuals you might use to support the ideas or enhance your presentation.

Idea 1:	Evidence, Examples, Elaboration:	Ideas for Visuals
Idea 2:	Evidence, Examples, Elaboration:	Ideas for Visuals
Idea 3:	Evidence, Examples, Elaboration:	Ideas for Visuals
Idea 4:	Evidence, Examples, Elaboration:	Ideas for Visuals

* Note that the number of points for the body of a presentation varies widely according to the topic and length of the presentation.

Name _____

Date _____ Class _____

Conclusion

Ideas for Visuals for Your Conclusion:

How will you restate and reinforce your thesis and show why it matters?

Handout 24A: Free African Society Notes

Directions: Use your note-taking skills to record key facets of the FAS's role in the epidemic. Then, analyze Murphy's depiction.

FAS Background and Connection to Dr. Rush (47–50)	Status of Black Philadelphians (48–50)	FAS Actions (50–51)	Responses to the FAS (51–52)	Scope of the FAS (53)
Key Details:	Key Details:	Key Details:	Key Details:	Key Details:

How is the FAS depicted? What methods does Murphy use to depict their motivation for volunteering?

Handout 25A: "Invictus" Analysis

Directions: Analyze the poem by completing the graphic organizer.

Word Bank: *metaphor, imagery, personification, rhyme*

Poem Vocabulary
fell: ruthless or vicious.
wince: to suddenly move away, as if in pain or distress.
bludgeonings: beatings inflicted by a heavy object.
menace: a dangerous person or thing.

1. Write a one- or two-sentence summary of each stanza in your own words.	1) 2) 3) 4)	
2. What can you infer about the speaker? Which quotations support your inferences?	1–2 Inferences:	Evidence:
3. Which *Fever 1793* character is most similar to the speaker? Support your response with evidence from the poem and *Fever 1793*.		

Handout 25B: Research Essay Model

Directions: Annotate the model to identify everything you notice about a research essay's structure.

Upper Class in Crisis

Imagine waking up in your city and noticing a pool of black vomit has stained your clothes. Imagine sick neighbors lying in your street. Imagine a city where farmers are so afraid to enter that citizens starve because food is scarce and expensive. Now, imagine being able to escape this city. That's what most wealthy citizens did during Philadelphia's yellow fever epidemic of 1793, though there were also wealthy heroes who stayed to help. Wealthy people experienced the epidemic differently because their resources gave them options. Most of the upper class responded by fleeing, which allowed them to survive, but resulted in some harmful effects on the city. Still, some wealthy citizens stayed behind and helped others.

20,000 Fled

Most wealthy people fled Philadelphia. This response helped wealthy families because it was the only way to ensure their children and loved ones could survive. In fact, "20,000 people abandoned the city during the fever" (Murphy 23). Since the entire city's population was only 51,000 (Murphy 3), almost half of Philadelphia ran away in the face of the yellow fever epidemic, proving that escaping was what anyone who had the resources did. Polak gives the example of Matthew Carey, who wrote journals discussing his commitment to stay in the city. However, even he "did abandon his fellow citizens for a time" because the fever was so dangerous. Likewise, government leaders fled to their country homes. The senators and representatives realized how vulnerable they were on the day they gathered to reassure citizens, and arrived at the state house to find Joseph Frye, the doorkeeper, dead. Murphy explains that Frye "had breathed the same air they were breathing now" (36). Congress adjourned even though problems resulted when the government essentially shut down. This example shows how typical it was for people to protect themselves and flee if they had the resources to do so.

Philadelphia Suffered

When upper-class citizens fled, they left behind poverty and suffering, worsening the problems in Philadelphia. Their flight was harmful even though it may have been necessary for survival. Murphy explains, "as well-off citizens closed their businesses and fled the city, they left behind thousands of individuals without any sort of income" (38). Citizens left behind in poverty lacked money for basic goods, food, and medical care. Polak's article emphasizes the suffering of these poor citizens. She states that the wealthy people who fled "left their more steadfast colleagues and the poor to fend for themselves." Her contrast reveals a critical tone because she compares people who fled to "more steadfast" citizens. Polak also uses an eyewitness account to show that at the epidemic's beginning, when wealthy citizens first fled, the Bush Hill hospital was "a great human slaughterhouse." This description shows the horror and dysfunction that occurred when so many of the citizens with resources abandoned Philadelphia.

The Heroic Few

On the other hand, some wealthy people stayed in the city and used their resources to help others. Mayor Clarkson led the city when the rest of the government fled, Israel Israel formed committees to aid the poor, and Stephen Girard transformed Bush Hill into a functioning hospital. Girard was considered "America's most powerful banker" when he undertook managing Bush Hill (DiMeo). A Philadelphian writer named Banneker stated that managing the hospital "seemed like an immediate sacrifice to the lives of the undertakers" (Polak). Girard was heroic for dedicating his resources to managing the hospital instead of escaping as so many of his neighbors chose to do. Murphy uses the testimony of an eyewitness who saw a victim vomit on Girard, "and Girard just comforted him" (Murphy 74). This emphasizes Girard's helpful response. "Bush Hill became a pocket of calm and hope" (Murphy 76) as a result of Girard's hard work, which makes Girard an excellent example of how some members of the upper class responded to the epidemic by helping others.

Conclusion

Most of the upper class fled the fever, but some wealthy people used their resources to stay behind to help other citizens access medical care and survive. Escaping had both helpful and harmful effects on the city. It was the only way wealthy citizens could protect themselves and their families. If wealthy people had not fled, a much higher percentage of Philadelphia's population might have died. However, when they fled, poverty increased and the most vulnerable citizens were left to suffer. It was fortunate that some wealthy people stayed to help others. In a crisis, most people are afraid, some take advantage of the sick, and some, like Stephen Girard, dedicate themselves to the greater good. It's important to understand the variety of options for responding to a crisis, because if Hurricane Katrina or the Ebola virus are any indication, there will always be another one to face.

Works Cited

DiMeo, Mike. "Stephen Girard." *Ushistory.org*. Independence Hall Association, Web. Accessed 6 Dec. 2016

Murphy, Jim. *An American Plague: The True and Terrifying Story of the Yellow Fever Epidemic of 1793*. New York: Clarion Books, 2003. Print.

Polak, Katherine. "Perspectives on Epidemic: The Yellow Fever in 1793 Philadelphia." *Constructing the Past*, vol. 5, issue 1, article 9, 2004.

Name _____

Date _____ Class _____

Handout 25C: Fluency Homework

Directions:

1. Day 1: Read the text carefully, and annotate to help you read fluently.
2. Each day:
   a. Practice reading the text aloud three to five times.
   b. Evaluate your progress by placing a check mark in the appropriate unshaded box.
   c. Ask someone (adult or peer) to listen and evaluate you as well.
3. Last day: Respond to the self-reflection questions at the end of this handout.

Invictus

Out of the night that covers me,

Black as the pit from pole to pole,

I thank whatever gods may be

For my unconquerable soul.

In the fell clutch of circumstance

I have not winced nor cried aloud.

Under the bludgeonings of chance

My head is bloody, but unbowed.

Beyond this place of wrath and tears

Looms but the Horror of the shade,

And yet the menace of the years

Finds and shall find me unafraid.

It matters not how strait the gate,

How charged with punishments the scroll,

I am the master of my fate,

I am the captain of my soul.

Henley, William Ernest. "Invictus." Poetry Foundation, Web. Accessed 6 Dec. 2016.

Student Performance Checklist:	Day 1		Day 2		Day 3		Day 4		Day 5	
	You	Listener*	You	Listener*	You	Listener*	You	Listener*	You	Listener*
Accurately read the passage three to five times.										
Read with appropriate phrasing and pausing.										
Read with appropriate expression.										
Read articulately at a good pace and an audible volume.										

*Adult or peer

Self-reflection: What choices did you make when deciding how to read this passage, and why? What would you like to improve on or try differently next time?

Name _____

Date _____ Class _____

Handout 27A: Speaking and Listening Goal-Setting and Self-Assessment

Directions: Use this tool to set a goal for and assess your participation in the Socratic Seminar by marking + for "yes" and Δ for "needs improvement" in the appropriate boxes.

Before the Discussion: Set a Goal

My goal for this discussion is to:

_____

_____

_____

After the Discussion: Self-Assess

Criteria	+/Δ
I came prepared for the discussion.	
I posed questions.	
I responded to questions.	
I made relevant observations.	
I acknowledged and built on others' ideas.	
I listened carefully.	
I brought the discussion back on topic as needed.	
I agreed and disagreed respectfully.	
• I did not interrupt.	
• I used a polite tone of voice.	
• I disagreed with the statement, not the person.	
I used appropriate, formal, academic language. For example:	

Criteria	+/Δ
I used vocabulary that I learned in this module, such as these words:	

I met my goal for this discussion. YES / NO

Explain:

_____

_____

_____

My goal for the next discussion is to:

_____

_____

_____

Name _____

Date _____   Class _____

Handout 28A: Character Analysis

Directions: Analyze any character from chapter 26 using textual evidence.

Character name _____

1. How is the character feeling in chapter 26? How does Anderson develop the character's point of view?	
2. How does the crisis affect this character?	

3. Identify and explain one *social factor* that impacts this character's experience of the crisis. (For example, age, race, class, or gender.)	
4. Based on this character's response to the crisis, how can you describe him or her?	

Handout 29A: Illness Words

Directions: Use the following as a reference throughout the vocabulary portion of the lesson.

Word	Meaning	Examples of Usage in the Texts
disease (n.)	A physical or mental condition that causes a part of the body (of a plant or animal) not to function correctly.	"Rush was never shy with his opinions, and standing there in the LeMaigres' parlor, he boldly announced that the disease they now confronted was the dreaded yellow fever" (Murphy 15).
epidemic (n.)	A rapid and widespread occurrence of disease.	"Almost all epidemics followed the same pattern, striking during warm weather, disappearing with the first hard frost" (Murphy 97).
fever (n.)	A body temperature that is higher than normal; a disease in which a high temperature is a central symptom.	"For on that Saturday a young French sailor rooming at Richard Denny's boarding house, over on North Water Street, was desperately ill with a fever" (Murphy 7). "Summer fevers were common visitors to all American cities in the eighteenth century, and therefore not headline news" (Murphy 9).
illness (n.)	Sickness or poor health.	"Putting the name yellow fever to the illness was not to be done lightly" (Murphy 15).
influenza (n.)	A respiratory infection, often referred to as flu.	"[Dr. Rush's] concern focused on a series of illnesses that had struck his patients throughout the year–the mumps in January, jaw and mouth infections in February, scarlet fever in March, followed by influenza in July" (Murphy 6).
grippe (n.)	A virus or flu.	"'I'm fine, child. I can wait until we get to the farm. I seem to have contracted a summer grippe'" (Anderson 82).
pestilence (n.)	A deadly illness or disease.	"Ricketts' was located in a quiet residential area many blocks away from the docks where the pestilence had first struck" (Murphy 39). "I tell you, William, men who stood unafraid before British cannon run in fear from this foul pestilence" (Anderson 60).
plague (n.)	A disease that spreads rapidly with a high death rate.	"Rush had, in short, announced that Philadelphia was in the grip of a deadly, unstoppable plague" (Murphy 16).
sickness (n.)	Illness or poor health.	"The sickness began with chills, headache, and a painful aching in the back, arms, and legs" (Murphy 13).

Name _____

Date _____ Class _____

Handout 30A: Aftermath Analysis

Directions: Revisit the following sections of *An American Plague*, and analyze the information to gain insight into power relations in eighteenth-century Philadelphia.

	What happened to members of this group in the epidemic's aftermath?	What do these specific examples reveal about *power relations*?
Government leaders (114–115)	Two or three examples:	
The lower class (114–115)	Two or three examples:	
The black community (117–122)	Two or three examples:	

How does this section of *An American Plague* influence your overall understanding of the epidemic?

Name _____

Date _____ Class _____

Handout 31A: Speaking and Listening Goal-Setting and Self-Assessment

Directions: Use this tool to set a goal for and assess your participation in the Socratic Seminar by marking + for "yes" and Δ for "needs improvement" in the appropriate boxes.

Before the Discussion: Set a Goal

My goal for this discussion is to:

_____
_____
_____

After the Discussion: Self-Assess

Criteria	+/Δ
I came prepared for the discussion.	
I posed questions.	
I responded to questions.	
I made relevant observations.	
I acknowledged and built on others' ideas.	
I listened carefully.	
I brought the discussion back on topic as needed.	
I agreed and disagreed respectfully.	
• I did not interrupt.	
• I used a polite tone of voice.	
• I disagreed with the statement, not the person.	
I used appropriate, formal, academic language. For example:	

Criteria	+/Δ
I used vocabulary that I learned in this module, such as these words:	

I met my goal for this discussion.   YES   /   NO

Explain:

_____
_____
_____

My goal for the next discussion is to:

_____
_____
_____

Handout 32A: Focusing Question Task 3 Organizer

Directions: Record evidence from *An American Plague* that you can use in a short essay explaining one thing that Philadelphians learned about their society as a result of the crisis.

After the crisis, what was one thing that people learned about their society?

Use bullet points to identify four or five details that would be useful to your response.	Explain how these details helped Philadelphians learn the lesson you identified above.

Handout 33A: End-of-Module Task Evidence

Directions: Record information in response to the research question: How did members of your selected group respond to the yellow fever crisis? Were these responses helpful, harmful, or both?

Topic: _____

Actions of your group members during the crisis	Supporting quotation or paraphrase (with citation)	Was this action helpful? How so?	Was this action harmful? How so?

Actions of your group members during the crisis	Supporting quotation or paraphrase (with citation)	Was this action helpful? How so?	Was this action harmful? How so?

Handout 34A: End-of-Module Task Evidence

Directions: Record information in response to the research question: How did members of your chosen group respond to the yellow fever crisis? Were these responses helpful, harmful, or both?

Topic: _____

Actions of your group members during the crisis	Supporting quotation or paraphrase (with citation)	Was this action helpful? How so?	Was this action harmful? How so?

Actions of your group members during the crisis	Supporting quotation or paraphrase (with citation)	Was this action helpful? How so?	Was this action harmful? How so?

Name _____

Date _____ Class _____

Handout 34B: Works Cited Guide

Directions: Credit writers and avoid plagiarism by citing sources and including a works cited page at the end of your essay. Many tools exist online for helping students determine how to cite sources! Use them, and review this guide to see MLA guidelines, one style for citing sources. While works can be cited in different ways, the important thing is to be consistent and provide readers with enough information that they can locate the sources themselves.

Be sure to cite:

- Another person's theory or idea.
- Information that is not common knowledge, such as statistics.
- Words spoken or written by someone else.

In-Text Citations

To cite within your essay, identify the author's name and page number in parenthesis (Murphy 25). If there is no author information, use the article title ("Philadelphia Fever").

Works Cited Page

Many sources provide their own citation information. If you are sure it is in the format we are using, you may copy and paste onto your works cited document.

Use this format for:

Online Source Citation:

Author or editor last name, first name. "Title of Article." *Title of Web Site*, Version (if available), Number (if available), Publisher, Publication Date, Location. Date of Access.

Example:

Paddock, Catharine. "Yellow Fever Research Breakthrough Could Lead to Better Treatment." *Medical News Today*, MediLexicon, Intl., 24 Nov. 2014. Accessed 8 Oct. 2015.

Book Citation:

Author last name, first name. *Title of Book*. Publisher, Publication Date.

Example:

Murphy, Jim. *An American Plague: The True and Terrifying Story of the Yellow Fever Epidemic of 1793*. Houghton Mifflin Harcourt, 2003.

Name _____

Date _____ Class _____

Handout 37A: Informative Essay Checklist

Directions: Use this checklist to evaluate and revise the draft. Mark a "**+**" to indicate that the writer has met the criterion. Mark a "Δ" to indicate the need for a change.

Reading Comprehension	Self +/Δ	Peer +/Δ	Teacher +/Δ
I clearly explain two to three ways members of my selected group responded to the yellow fever crisis, and I evaluate whether these responses were helpful, harmful, or both.			
I show that I understand what happened during the yellow fever crisis of 1793.			
Structure			
I respond to all parts of the prompt.			
I focus on my topic throughout the piece.			
I introduce the topic clearly in my introduction paragraph, giving a preview of the rest of the essay.			
I organize my ideas clearly in body paragraphs.			
My conclusion paragraph supports the focus.			
I use transitions to smoothly and logically connect paragraphs and ideas.			
I use headings or graphics to aid comprehension.			
Development			
I develop the topic with sufficient evidence from *An American Plague* and at least two other credible sources.			
My evidence is smoothly incorporated and relevant to the topic.			
I elaborate upon evidence by analyzing it accurately.			
Style			
I use a variety of sentence patterns (simple, compound, compound-complex) to add clarity and interest to my writing.			
I use vocabulary words that are specific and appropriate to the content.			
I write precisely and concisely, without using unnecessary words.			
I write in a formal style that is appropriate for the audience.			

Conventions			
I spell correctly.			
I use appropriate transitions (phrases and clauses) within and among paragraphs to connect ideas.			
I use commas to separate coordinate adjectives.			
I use technology to cite sources consistently and correctly.			

To Be Completed by the Peer Reviewer

Peer Reviewer Name:

Praise:

Suggestion:

Name

Date   Class

Handout 38A: Speaking and Listening Goal-Setting and Self-Assessment

Directions: Use this tool to set a goal for and assess your participation in the Socratic Seminar by marking + for "yes" and Δ for "needs improvement" in the appropriate boxes.

Before the Discussion: Set a Goal

My goal for this discussion is to:

_____

_____

_____

After the Discussion: Self-Assess

Criteria	+/Δ
I came prepared for the discussion.	
I posed questions.	
I responded to questions.	
I made relevant observations.	
I acknowledged and built on others' ideas.	
I listened carefully.	
I brought the discussion back on topic as needed.	
I agreed and disagreed respectfully.	
▪ I did not interrupt.	
▪ I used a polite tone of voice.	
▪ I disagreed with the statement, not the person.	
I used appropriate, formal, academic language. For example:	

Criteria	+/Δ
I used vocabulary that I learned in this module, such as these words:	

I met my goal for this discussion.   YES   /   NO

Explain:

_____

_____

_____

My goal for the future discussions is to:

_____

_____

_____

Volume of Reading Reflection Questions

Fever, Grade 7, Module 4

Student Name: _____

Text: _____

Author: _____

Topic: _____

_____

Genre/Type of Book: _____

Share your knowledge by answering the questions or responding to the prompts below.

Informational Texts

1. **Wonder:** What drew you to read this informational text? Cite three things you noticed or wondered during your first read.
2. **Organize:** Summarize the text.
3. **Reveal:** Choose a section of the text. Explain how this section fit into the overall structure of the text. Explain how this section helps the reader understand the big idea.
4. **Distill:** What is the essential meaning of this text? What does this essential meaning show about the author's point of view?
5. **Know:** How does this text's information add to what you already know about this topic? Describe a book that has information on a similar topic. Tell how the two books are similar and different.
6. **Vocabulary:** Write and define three words in this text that are important to understanding the topic or ideas. Explain what strategy was most helpful to define the words (context, roots or affixes, or a dictionary).

Literary Texts

1. **Wonder:** After reading the first few pages of the text, what observations can you make? What questions do you have?
2. **Organize:** Summarize the story, including the main character(s), setting, conflict, and resolution. Tell how the setting shapes the plot.

3. **Reveal:** Explore the setting of this literary work. Find a historical account of the same period. How close are the historical details? How much does the fictional work use or alter historical details to tell a story? Support your answer with details from the text.

4. **Distill:** What is a theme of this story? How does it develop over the course of the text?

5. **Know:** How does this text build your knowledge? Support your response with details from this text.

6. **Vocabulary:** Identify and define three words that were new to you with this text and that were used in an interesting way to describe the character or setting or tell the story. Explain what strategy was most helpful to define the words (context, roots or affixes, or a dictionary).

WIT & WISDOM PARENT TIP SHEET

WHAT IS MY GRADE 7 STUDENT LEARNING IN MODULE 4?

Wit & Wisdom is our English curriculum. It builds knowledge of key topics in history, science, and literature through the study of excellent texts. By reading and responding to stories and nonfiction texts, we will build knowledge of the following topics:

Module 1: Identity in the Middle Ages

Module 2: Americans All

Module 3: Language and Power

Module 4: Fever

In the fourth module, *Fever*, students explore a powerful moment in American history, the yellow fever epidemic in Philadelphia in 1793, and use this crisis to explore human responses and to ask and investigate research questions. Throughout, students ask: *How can times of crisis affect citizens and society?*

OUR CLASS WILL READ AND VIEW THESE TEXTS:

Novel (Literary)

- *Fever 1793*, Laurie Halse Anderson

Historical Account

- *An American Plague*, Jim Murphy

Painting

- *The Artist in His Museum*, Charles Willson Peale

Websites

- "Yellow Fever," U.S. National Library of Medicine
- "Q&A," Jim Murphy

Video

- *Philadelphia: The Great Experiment*, History Making Productions

OUR CLASS WILL ASK THESE QUESTIONS:

- In what context did the yellow fever epidemic of 1793 emerge?
- What were the effects of the unfolding crisis on Philadelphia and its citizens?
- What did the crisis reveal about Philadelphia's citizens and society?
- How did people respond to the crisis?
- What is the story of the year?

QUESTIONS TO ASK AT HOME:

As your Grade 7 student reads, ask:

- What have you learned about the crisis and the response to it?
- How does what you are reading build your knowledge of how people and societies handle crisis?
- What do the books you are reading show about historical research?

BOOKS TO READ AT HOME:

- *Invisible Microbe: Tuberculosis and the Never-Ending Search for a Cure*, Jim Murphy
- *Oh, Rats! The Story of Rats and People*, Albert Marrin
- *Terrible Typhoid Mary: A True Story of the Deadliest Cook in America*, Susan Campbell Bartoletti
- *When Plague Strikes: The Black Death, Smallpox, AIDS*, James Cross Giblin
- *The Great Trouble: A Mystery of London, the Blue Death, and a Boy Called Eel*, Deborah Hopkinson

IDEAS FOR DISCUSSING HISTORY AND CRISES:

The core texts in this module help students see different human responses to a crisis and the importance of historical knowledge and research to accurately depict history. Discuss historical events and people and past and modern-day crises, as well as the responses to those crises. Ask questions such as:

1. For history: The study of history helps us to understand not only our past but our present. Read history books together, and share stories about your personal history. Help students see how the past informs the present—and how we can learn from the past.

2. For crises: Read other related books or the news together and discuss the contexts, causes, events, and effects of crises. Help your student see that individual actions can make a difference and that people can respond compassionately and courageously in response to natural or human-made disasters.

3. For all content: Encourage your child to ask questions, and when he or she does, work together to investigate and research the answers to those questions.

CREDITS

Great Minds® has made every effort to obtain permission for the reprinting of all copyrighted material. If any owner of copyrighted material is not acknowledged herein, please contact Great Minds® for proper acknowledgment in all future editions and reprints of this module.

- All material from the *Common Core State Standards for English Language Arts & Literacy in History/Social Studies, Science, and Technical Subjects* © Copyright 2010 National Governors Association Center for Best Practices and Council of Chief State School Officers. All rights reserved.
- All images are used under license from Shutterstock.com unless otherwise noted.
- For updated credit information, please visit **http://witeng.link/credits**.

ACKNOWLEDGMENTS

Great Minds® Staff

The following writers, editors, reviewers, and support staff contributed to the development of this curriculum.

Ann Brigham, Lauren Chapalee, Sara Clarke, Emily Climer, Lorraine Griffith, Emily Gula, Sarah Henchey, Trish Huerster, Stephanie Kane-Mainier, Lior Klirs, Liz Manolis, Andrea Minich, Lynne Munson, Marya Myers, Rachel Rooney, Aaron Schifrin, Danielle Shylit, Rachel Stack, Sarah Turnage, Michelle Warner, Amy Wierzbicki, Margaret Wilson, and Sarah Woodard.

Colleagues and Contributors

We are grateful for the many educators, writers, and subject-matter experts who made this program possible.

David Abel, Robin Agurkis, Elizabeth Bailey, Julianne Barto, Amy Benjamin, Andrew Biemiller, Charlotte Boucher, Sheila Byrd-Carmichael, Eric Carey, Jessica Carloni, Janine Cody, Rebecca Cohen, Elaine Collins, Tequila Cornelious, Beverly Davis, Matt Davis, Thomas Easterling, Jeanette Edelstein, Kristy Ellis, Moira Clarkin Evans, Charles Fischer, Marty Gephart, Kath Gibbs, Natalie Goldstein, Christina Gonzalez, Mamie Goodson, Nora Graham, Lindsay Griffith, Brenna Haffner, Joanna Hawkins, Elizabeth Haydel, Steve Hettleman, Cara Hoppe, Ashley Hymel, Carol Jago, Jennifer Johnson, Mason Judy, Gail Kearns, Shelly Knupp, Sarah Kushner, Shannon Last, Suzanne Lauchaire, Diana Leddy, David Liben, Farren Liben, Jennifer Marin, Susannah Maynard, Cathy McGath, Emily McKean, Jane Miller, Rebecca Moore, Cathy Newton, Turi Nilsson, Julie Norris, Galemarie Ola, Michelle Palmieri, Meredith Phillips, Shilpa Raman, Tonya Romayne, Emmet Rosenfeld, Jennifer Ruppel, Mike Russoniello, Deborah Samley, Casey Schultz, Renee Simpson, Rebecca Sklepovich, Amelia Swabb, Kim Taylor, Vicki Taylor, Melissa Thomson, Lindsay Tomlinson, Melissa Vail, Keenan Walsh, Julia Wasson, Lynn Welch, Yvonne Guerrero Welch, Emily Whyte, Lynn Woods, and Rachel Zindler.

Early Adopters

The following early adopters provided invaluable insight and guidance for Wit & Wisdom:

- Bourbonnais School District 53 • Bourbonnais, IL
- Coney Island Prep Middle School • Brooklyn, NY
- Gate City Charter School for the Arts • Merrimack, NH
- Hebrew Academy for Special Children • Brooklyn, NY
- Paris Independent Schools • Paris, KY
- Saydel Community School District • Saydel, IA
- Strive Collegiate Academy • Nashville, TN
- Valiente College Preparatory Charter School • South Gate, CA
- Voyageur Academy • Detroit, MI

Design Direction provided by Alton Creative, Inc.
Project management support, production design, and copyediting services provided by ScribeConcepts.com
Copyediting services provided by Fine Lines Editing
Product management support provided by Sandhill Consulting